Payc

An Apprentice Eternal

Brad Allen DeBorde

Paydunor

An Apprentice Eternal

Characters

Queen Larrel, 50's, elegant

Lady Elisven (Ellie), 18, the Queen's ward

The Magistrate, 50's, pompous and dastardly

Lady Sisk, 30, a Necromancer, jaded and cruel

Fenian,17 and meek, but with a light optimism that shines through the dark, apprentice to Sisk

Tofol, elderly, funny and wizened

Wren, immortal, a demon and servant to Tofol

Ferra, timeless and ageless, a healer

Anna,17 and sassy, assistant to Ferra

Lorason,18 Ademar's squire, young and brash

Ademar, 30, a knight

Servants, knights, people of court

Act I

*(Morning in the entry hall of the Marble Castle.
The **QUEEN** enters. She is wearing a long gown that
trails behind her. She is followed by The **MAGISTRATE**.
He is in a fine long robe with a chain of office.)*

QUEEN

Any other business we need to discuss, Magistrate?

MAGISTRATE

Yes, Your Majesty. I am happy to report that
our scouts have seen your guests trekking this way
from across Paydunor. Tofol, the collector, Lady
Sisk, the necromancer and Ademar, the knight. Each
bringing with them their protégés as requested.

QUEEN

Very good. I am excited to meet with them all.
But that is just three of the four queries that were
sent. Where is our fourth guest?

MAGISTRATE

I fear we received no response from the fourth,
Your Majesty.

QUEEN

Pity. I had high hopes that all my invitations
would have yielded a visit.

MAGISTRATE

I'm sure no disrespect was meant. Perhaps something has kept them from their journey.

QUEEN

Perhaps. *(Pause.)* The King would have enjoyed this day.

MAGISTRATE

Would he? I didn't know the King to have enjoyed magicians and charlatans parading their lies about the castle.

QUEEN

Your prejudice is showing, Magistrate.

MAGISTRATE

My apologies, Your Highness.

QUEEN

My husband enjoyed learning about the powers the citizens of Paydunor possessed. Not only magic, but he admired strength and knowledge.

MAGISTRATE

I wish more of humanity were as impressive as your late husband, my Queen. He was a man I truly admired.

QUEEN

Did you have such a high regard for him?

MAGISTRATE

Yes, Your Majesty. His courage in battles, his diplomacy—all great qualities I strive to possess.

QUEEN

Maybe you and the council should start referring to my husband's deeds before declaring new laws and sanctions on the people of the East? Rule by his paradigm.

MAGISTRATE

Your Majesty, we—

QUEEN

Show me you truly admire him, Magistrate. Be an example.

MAGISTRATE

Of course, Your Highness.

*(**ELLIE** enters and curtsies to the **QUEEN**.)*

ELLIE

Your Majesty.

QUEEN

Ellie, my dear. Come, stand with me as we wait for our guests.

MAGISTRATE

I will take my leave.

*(The **MAGISTRATE** bows and exits. **ELLIE** walks over to the **QUEEN**.)*

ELLIE

How are you feeling today?

QUEEN

Better than yesterday, but still weak. I think the excitement of the day has given me a burst of energy.

ELLIE

How lovely. I am glad to hear it. Have you eaten today?

QUEEN

We must discuss what you will wear today.

ELLIE

You are avoiding the question.

QUEEN

Yes, my dear. I have eaten.

ELLIE

Good. I have it on good authority that you didn't yesterday. That may explain why you are so weak this morning. I hope I am not too bold in saying so, your Majesty?

QUEEN

Not at all. It brings me comfort knowing you are concerned for my well-being. How are you today?

ELLIE

Admittedly a bit anxious.

QUEEN

Anxious?

ELLIE

It isn't every day you are presented with potential suitors.

QUEEN

So you found out about my hidden intentions?

ELLIE

Your intentions were not hidden very well, Your Grace.

QUEEN

Well, I am sad to say it is just one suitor now, as one of the four invited guests is not likely to come.

ELLIE

I am sorry to hear that. I know you have your heart set on this meeting.

QUEEN

Not just my heart, child, but this kingdom's future. New Trale has been a beacon of prosperity and I shudder to think what might become of Paydunor when I am gone. The Three seem to ignore my prayers, our relations with Poneleve are still teetering on the brink of collapsing into war and the Magistrate's influence continues to gain momentum.

ELLIE

I am sorry…

QUEEN

It is not your fault. I took you in as ward to raise you away from demons and tainted bloodlines. You were a peace offering and a gift I still cherish to this day. You being here keeps all of Paydunor at peace.

ELLIE

I thought it was you who kept the peace?

QUEEN

Only because I have you, dear. That is why I want you to marry soon. Before I am gone.

ELLIE

Gone? I don't like hearing you speak of such dark things.

QUEEN

My time is limited.

ELLIE

My Queen, your mind is as sharp and witty as ever. Physically, you seem to be harming yourself. You sleep only an hour or two a night and I rarely see you eat. I see nothing that tells me you are ill other than that you are tired and malnourished.

QUEEN

I feel it. It fluctuates, but I feel it. A sickness. That is why I urge you to keep the kingdom safe by marrying. When wed, I can legally make you my heir and successor to the crown. 'If the crown looks to lose a royal line…

ELLIE

-then the crown falls to the council of the nine.' I have heard this many times, my Queen. It is an outdated law and one that holds no merit.

(Pause.)

I will meet with your suitor today. I must say, meeting one rather than several is a comfort.

QUEEN

Thank you, Ellie. That brings me some relief.

ELLIE

I hope I can help, Your Grace.

QUEEN

I have faith that you will. Now, show me to my room, please.

ELLIE

Yes, Your Majesty.

*(The two exit. A beat passes. **SISK** enters. She is in long black robes.)*

SISK

Ah, the Marble Castle. Stunning. Absolutely stunning. Come along, Fenian. Be careful with those vials and other pouches. Their contents are worth more than your life. No. Let me re-phrase that. I care more about their contents than I do your life.

*(**FENIAN** enters dressed in a simple vest and pants. He has a patch on his vest of a vial indicating that he belongs to **SISK**. He is carrying several leather bags that clink with glass.)*

FENIAN

Yes, m'lady.

SISK

Sometimes I feel you don't quite understand how unimportant you really are in the grand scheme of life, Fenian.

FENIAN

Am I not a suitable apprentice, m'lady?

SISK

I hope that was not a note of sarcasm in your voice just now.

FENIAN

No, m'lady. I was serious in my inquiry. Is there more I could do? I am willing to learn and…

SISK

I will inform you when I see potential for improvement. Is that really the best you had to wear?

FENIAN

To wear?

SISK

Yes. Look at where we are, boy. The greatest and most lavish castle in all of Paydunor and you are dressed as… as…

FENIAN

An apprentice?

SISK

Do not be smart with me.

FENIAN

Yes, m'lady. The truth is, m'lady, I had only one other set of clothes you were gracious enough to buy me, but I have since grown out of them.

SISK

Perhaps you should stop growing? There is a draught in that satchel there that might help. Here, let me give you just two-

FENIAN

No, m'lady, please. I meant no disrespect.

SISK

If all goes as I hope while we are here I can afford to buy you many more outfits. Then perhaps I won't be too embarrassed to be seen with you.

FENIAN

I would be thankful.

SISK

Now, do you remember what I told you before we left the Tower?

FENIAN

(Reciting) We have had several successes with lower beings, such as Goblins and demons. We hope the Queen will allow us the honor of being the first royal to undergo our treatment.

SISK

And the cost of my services?

FENIAN

Land and Title as well as a place at court.

SISK

Very good. Set the bags in that corner there and make yourself presentable.

FENIAN

Yes, m'lady.

SISK

You also know your part to play in this?

FENIAN

I am to get to know the Lady Elisven.

SISK

Yes. She is of age and ready to marry. If I can secure our place in court, maybe you can secure our future. I have taught you how to bow and present yourself, yes? (*FENIAN nods.*) Good. I know I can sometimes be unkind to you, Fenian, but do not think that is always the case. Look in that leather bag for the item wrapped in red paper. (*FENIAN does as she asks.*) Open it.

FENIAN

Is this a gift?

SISK

Yes.

(*FENIAN opens the paper to find a magnificent hat. He places it on his head.*)

Very handsome, I must say. Even rusted copper can be polished.

FENIAN

Thank you, Lady Sisk. I am undeserving of such a beautiful gift.

SISK

You are, yes, but dressing yourself with such plumage may win you the favor of Lady Elisven. You aren't the most unattractive young man she will have met. Just try not to talk too much.

FENIAN

Yes, m'lady.

SISK

Now show me a proper bow. *(He does so. Pause.)* I suppose that will suffice.

FENIAN

Lady Sisk?

SISK

What is it?

FENIAN

What does one say when talking to…

SISK

When talking to women?

FENIAN

Yes, m'Lady. Have you ever been wooed? What was said that made you…

SISK

I was wooed once, yes. I was once treated kindly. We talked about travel and dreams. All sweet words and secret desires.

FENIAN

What happened?

SISK

The same thing that happens to most young romances. It died as quickly as it sprang into being.

(Pause.)

But, that won't happen to you. If you can get close to the Queen's ward, I suspect you will fall madly in love and stay there blissfully until the end of the age, despite your shortcomings.

*(The **MAGISTRATE** enters.)*

MAGISTRATE

Lady Sisk! (*He bows.*) What a pleasure it is to see you on this fine morning. I do hope the travel from Poneleve was pleasant?

SISK

It was tolerable. Is there a room where my apprentice can setup my equipment?

MAGISTRATE

Not yet, my Lady.

SISK

It takes time to prep the ingredients. If the Queen is in a hurry and it sounded as if…

MAGISTRATE

The Queen wants to hear all of her options before letting anyone implement their trade. This is the royal bloodline we are trying to save.

SISK

I hear the blood line is what you are trying to drain, good sir. Let me have a room to at least unpack my equipment.

MAGISTRATE

You wound me with your words, Lady Sisk. I do want to see a council represent the good people of New Trale, but I would never wish for harm to befall Her Grace. The Queen is a kind ruler and her people have been prosperous under her rule.

SISK

Then why wish for a change in leadership, sir?

MAGISTRATE

I look to the future and see the disaster rising in the east. My thoughts and intentions are not hidden from the public. I am quite open about my distaste for the…

SISK

The mages?

MAGISTRATE

Queen Larrel sympathizes with their plight. I see them for what they truly are: abominations; corrupted by their own maladies and sickness which they call gifts. I, and the council, when in power will not rest until…

FENIAN

It is not a sickness!

SISK

Insolent boy! How dare you speak to the Magistrate in this manner!

FENIAN

But you yourself have…

SISK

Quiet! (*She smacks him.* **FENIAN** *falls to the ground.*) Speak out of turn again and I will use your own life to bring back one which is lost. (*She turns back to the* **MAGISTRATE**.) I am sorry for my apprentice. The boy is troubled in the head. He has seen many lives lost and returned. It can affect one's sense of reality.

MAGISTRATE

No apologies necessary. I understand that the boy must have witnessed many horrors, real and otherwise, working for a necromancer.

(**TOFOL** *enters. He wears great blue robes and has a long white beard. He is followed by* **WREN***, a demon. The demon has scaled skin and wears an ornate tail-coat over ragged shirt and pant.*)

TOFOL

Well, it has been awhile since I have set foot in this magnificent place. It hasn't changed in my great absence. Ah, Magistrate, I am happy to meet you finally after such a long correspondence. Wren, place my things with the young boy over there. I am sure he will see them to a room.

FENIAN

I don't actually…

TOFOL

It is alright, my boy. Here is a silver for your troubles. (*Hands* **FENIAN** *a coin.*)

FENIAN

No, sir, it's just that…

SISK

He works for me, sir.

TOFOL.

Ah. Keep the silver then as an apology.

FENIAN

Thank you, sir!

SISK

I'll be taking that.

TOFOL

(*To* **SISK.**) I do not believe we have met.

SISK

We have not. I am Lady Sisk. (*She bows.*)

TOFOL

Sick, you say?

SISK

Sisk.

TOFOL

You don't feel well?

SISK

SISK! LADY SISK!

TOFOL

The necromancer?

SISK

The same, yes.

TOFOL

My name is Tofol. Master of Items of Antiquity. Lady Sisk, I gave that silver to the young man. It is his.

SISK

He is under my employ, what he earns goes to me.

TOFOL

It was a gift then. Nothing earned.

SISK

Very well, then. He can use it to buy some new clothes.

TOFOL

Let me introduce you to my associate, Wren.

MAGISTRATE

A demon? Here? Do you not know of the tension between the two kingdoms of New Trale and Poneleve?

TOFOL

I do, yes. Wren is not under any control, I can assure you.

MAGISTRATE

His presence may cause panic.

TOFOL

He shall stay by my side at all times. Now shake my hand and welcome me! (*TOFOL extends his hand to MAGISTRATE.*) I feel as if we are longtime estranged friends.

MAGISTRATE

(*Taking TOFOL's hand.*) I hope I can trust you as one trusts a longtime friend. Your hand, sir, is cold as the Northern rains. Are you well?

TOFOL

Yes, I am sorry, these old hands do not get the

greatest of circulation. Is the Queen about? I would love to meet with her.

MAGISTRATE

She has requested meeting everyone at the same time here in the great hall within the hour. I however have a room set up for you, sir.

SISK

(*Indignantly.*) The old man has a room and I do not?

MAGISTRATE

He has other business here than what you were called to do.

TOFOL

Yes, Lady Sisk, I am taking this opportunity to study in the library here for several days. The Queen and Magistrate saw to my request. Did you not ask for accommodations when replying to the royal summons?

(*SISK ignores his question.*)

Pity. It's always good to think ahead, My Lady. Now show me to my room, good Magistrate.

MAGISTRATE

Of course! This way please.

TOFOL

Come along, Wren.

(*MAGISTRATE begins to lead TOFOL and WREN off stage.*)

SISK

The old man has a room and I am to wait out here in the entry hall like a…

MAGISTRATE

I do apologize. This may seem rude, but Tofol is here on other business.

SISK

So you both have said.

TOFOL

And these old bones must find time to rest.

SISK

Perhaps I may find a way to have them rest forever, sir.

TOFOL

You wouldn't be very good at your trade if you make good on that jape.

(**SISK** turns in anger as the **MAGISTRATE, TOFOL** and **WREN** exit.)

SISK

How dare they treat me this way!

FENIAN

I am sorry, m'lady, but he does seem to have other matters to attend to than that of the Queen.

(*SISK strikes FENIAN again.*)

SISK

You need to learn not to talk out of turn! I am off to find an empty space in this marble monstrosity. Stay here and do not move.

FENIAN

(*Cowering a bit.*) Yes, m'lady.

(*SISK exits. FENIAN sits up and begins to stack the luggage in a better pile. ELLIE enters. FENIAN drops a vial and it rolls across the floor. He fumbles a bit before catching it. ELLIE laughs.*)

FENIAN

Oh! Hello. I am sorry. I didn't see you there.

ELLIE

I'm sorry, I should have announced myself. What have you got there?

FENIAN

I'm not sure. Most of the glassware is written in a language I haven't learned.

ELLIE

So it's a mystery? May I see it?

FENIAN

I'm not sure… Lady Sisk has never shared her secrets before. Nor has she-

ELLIE

I won't tell if you don't.

(*FENIAN* *smiles and hands it to her. She reads the label. She laughs.*)

It is only water and blue dye.

FENIAN

Is it?

ELLIE

See? (*FENIAN* *steps closer as she points to the vial.*) That is the Goblin symbol for blue and the demon symbol for water.

FENIAN

Wow. You can read other languages?

ELLIE

Don't be too impressed. These are just symbols I happen to recognize from an old children's book.

FENIAN

(*Taking the vial back.*) Why would Lady Sisk keep water with dye among the potions and powders?

ELLIE

Lady Sisk? Why does that name sound familiar?

FENIAN

The Necromancer?

ELLIE

Yes! That's where I know it from. She is one of the queen's guests.

FENIAN

I am her apprentice. Lady Sisk, that is. Not the

Queen's.

ELLIE

It would be rather odd to have a boy as a Queen's apprentice.

FENIAN

(To himself.) Why would she have blue water?

ELLIE

(Walking to the other bags and satchels.) Let's see what the other labels say.

FENIAN

(Getting between her and the Satchels.) NO!

(Pause.)

I'm sorry. I mean- I shouldn't-t- WE shouldn't be looking through Lady Sisk's bags. I have been punished for looking through her cabinets at the tower before. Her privacy is very important to her.

ELLIE

The Tower?

FENIAN

That is what she calls her lab. Our home. It is in a village, West of Poneleve on the Giant's Path. The village used to be large with a lot of people. But they have been leaving for the bigger cities. Lady Sisk's reputation is to blame, I think. The Tower is the last standing stone structure of a once great castle that was left to Lady Sisk by a client of hers.

ELLIE

It sounds magnificent.

FENIAN

It scares me to live in it. I'm not sure when it will fall.

ELLIE

If it falls, you mean?

FENIAN

What?

ELLIE

You're scared because you aren't sure if it will fall or not. That uncertainty is frightening.

FENIAN

Oh, no. I know it will fall. Knowing it will fall on top of me is what scares me.

ELLIE

(*Laughing.*) I'm sure it's more stable than you describe.

FENIAN

(*Shaking his head but laughing a bit with her.*) No, madam. It is a nightmare I have played out in my head on a daily basis. I am secretly hoping it crumbles while we are away.

ELLIE

Then you would have no place to live.

FENIAN

I'm sure we would find shelter on the road. Maybe even find a kinder village or move east and stay with the mages.

ELLIE

Well you best put away that blue water. You wouldn't want her to see you holding it.

FENIAN

True. Thank you for reminding me. Sometimes I slip into these little daydreams and forget that I'm holding something or supposed to be working.

ELLIE

I'm sure Lady Sisk looks poorly on that.

FENIAN

She does, yes. I have the bruises to prove it.

ELLIE

Is she a true necromancer?

FENIAN

I have seen her work. I have seen dark things. I have seen her revive animals and Goblins.

ELLIE

Do you think Lady Sisk can help the Queen?

FENIAN

I have seen her give life to those that have recently died. I have never seen her prevent death. Maybe she can bring the Queen back when the worse happens.

ELLIE

If the worst happens, you mean?

FENIAN

She is dying. I was told that she…

ELLIE

She thinks she is. I feel she is killing herself out of paranoia. I am hoping, once the Queen's options are laid out in front of her, she will wake from her fear and live life the way she once did.

FENIAN

You seem heavily invested in Her Majesty's well-being.

ELLIE

The whole of Paydunor should be heavily invested. If she dies, the council will seize control. Mages will go into hiding and the council's warped view of the Three will cause people to hate that which they once loved.

FENIAN

You know so much of the politics within the castle.

ELLIE

I hate knowing what I know. I wish I could just live in ignorance.

FENIAN

That isn't all it's cracked up to be either.

ELLIE

But you are learning a trade, right? That must be fascinating.

FENIAN

I wish I was learning more. Lady Sisk is so secretive. I am sometimes not even in the same room with her when she performs her spells or mixes her concoctions.

ELLIE

That is odd. I would think an apprentice would be by her side at all times.

FENIAN

Rarely. I have however been reading her books, the ones in the common tongue. I am beginning to get a grasp of the concept of-

(*MAGISTRATE enters.*)

MAGISTRATE

Lady Elisven, there you are, my dear.

FENIAN

(*Surprised.*) Lady Ell…

ELLIE

I have been here talking with our guests, Magistrate, but in our talks, I am afraid decorum has left us. Let us properly introduce ourselves, shall we. (*FENIAN nods.*) I am Lady Elisven Selvetarm. You may call me Ellie.

FENIAN

(*Bowing.*) I am Fenian, apprentice to Lady Sisk.

ELLIE

No last name?

FENIAN

Both of my parents are from Codac, m'lady. No last names.

ELLIE

A son of two mercenaries? Interesting. I am very pleased to meet you, Fenian.

MAGISTRATE

Have no other guests arrived, my lady?

ELLIE

Not to my knowledge, Magistrate. (*Indignant.*) Maybe the invitations were sent later than hoped?

MAGISTRATE

Is that an accusation, my lady?

ELLIE

Not at all, sir. I just hope that all got the word of the Queen's meeting so that they could coordinate getting here for Her Majesty's gathering.

MAGISTRATE

I am sure the Decrees of Invite made it into the proper hands.

ELLIE

(*Turning back to* **FENIAN**) I like your hat, sir. I noticed it earlier but I was too swept up in our conversation to say anything.

FENIAN

My hat? Oh, yes. Thank you, my lady.

ELLIE

It is very becoming.

FENIAN

It was a gift. (*Pause.*) Your dress is very become...

(**FERRA** *enters. She is wearing great green robes that trail behind her. She is beautiful and timeless. Her hair is wrapped and hidden under silks. Behind her is* **ANNA**. *She too wears green robes, but they are much shorter than that of her master's.*)

FERRA

(*Softly.*) It has been a long time since I have set foot in this castle. The Great Marble Castle. A historic day for humanity. Anna?

ANNA

Yes, Lady Ferra?

FERRA

Place our bag next to those in the corner. I am sure no room has been prepared for us.

MAGISTRATE

(*Disgusted.*) Ferra, the Healer. Nice to see that the open road agrees with you.

FERRA

Of course it does.

MAGISTRATE

No trouble I hope?

FERRA

(*Very calm.*) We were set upon by a group of thieves and cutthroats just before arriving at Riddon for the night. As they lay dying on the side of the road, they used their last breath to say that one of authority sent them to attack us.

MAGISTRATE

Did they?

FERRA

Yes, my dear Magistrate. Who would want to hurt a healer and her assistant?

MAGISTRATE

Who indeed.

FERRA

I hope we do not have to look over our shoulders too often while we stay here, sir? I hate feeling as if I am being watched or judged. (*Turning to **ELLIE**.*) This must be the Lady Elisven. I am pleased to meet you.

ELLIE

I am pleased to meet you. I have heard many phenomenal stories about your good deeds across

Paydunor.

FERRA

Stories, I am sure, told out of context to make me seem better than I truly am.

ELLIE

Some I have read in books. Documented by trusted historians.

FERRA

I am flattered you think so highly of me, Lady Elisven.

MAGISTRATE

There are other tales I have told Lady Elisven as well. Though, she doesn't take heed of their message.

ELLIE

I'm sure those dark tales are also born out of misplaced context and fear.

FERRA

(*Ignoring them and moving towards* **FENIAN**.) And you young man? What is your name and title?

FENIAN

Fenian, m'lady. I am apprentice to…

FERRA

Lady Sisk?

FENIAN

Yes.

FERRA

Take my hand, Fenian. (*He does so.*) I feel an abundance of warmth within you. It is building up to something great. I hope to be around to see you do amazing things.

FENIAN

Yes, m'lady.

FERRA

(*Turning back to the Magistrate.*) I saw Tofol enter the gates ahead of me. I would be grateful if I could meet with him.

MAGISTRATE

Perhaps. He is settling into his room.

FERRA

I'm sure he wouldn't mind some company.

MAGISTRATE

Of course, this way. (*He exits.*)

FERRA

Anna, stay with our things and get to know these two better.

ANNA

Of course, Lady Ferra.

(**FERRAA** *Exits.* **ANNA** *walks over to* **FENIAN** *and* **ELLIE.**)

ANNA

An apprentice to a necromancer… That must be interesting.

FENIAN

I guess.

ELLIE

I have suspicions she is a charlatan.

ANNA

Most who claim to restore life are fakes.

FENIAN

She is not a…

ANNA

My name is Anna.

ELLIE

My name is Ellie and this is Fenian.

ANNA

A queen's apprentice. What is that like?

ELLIE

Well, I guess the Queen has taken me as an apprentice. Officially I am her ward. But, let us drop our titles and just be friends, okay?

ANNA

I'd like that very much. Ferra isn't much for titles.

ELLIE

The Queen and Magistrate insist that we be formal around guests, but it is so tiring.

ANNA

I can imagine. (*She walks around a bit.*) This place is amazing. Have you explored this entire castle?

ELLIE

Most of it. I have never been to the lower levels. Too damp and cold. The higher levels have the better rooms. A library, a banquet hall and countless rooms decorated in the themes of the different regions of Paydunor.

ANNA

It sounds incredible. Maybe if our stay is extended, you can show me your favorite places here?

ELLIE

I would like that very much.

ANNA

What is the town like?

ELLIE

New Trale? Busy. Lots of shops and taverns and inns and… mostly just travelers and mercenaries.

ANNA

It must be nice to stay in one place all the time.

ELLIE

I am jealous of those who get to travel. I have seen only my home kingdom of Poneleve and here. We passed through Riddon while I slept, I didn't even get to see the small town. I was so young, though. I probably wouldn't even remember what it looked like had I seen it.

ANNA

Riddon has grown the past few years. It is a welcoming place where we stay for several days at a time. There is always work there.

ELLIE

Fenian, you are quiet. What places have you seen?

(*FENIAN doesn't respond.*)

ANNA

You may have upset him calling Lady Sisk a charlatan.

ELLIE

You're the one who brought up the idea. I merely agreed that those who claim to…

FENIAN

Lugent.

ELLIE

I'm sorry?

FENIAN

I have been to Lugent, to Poneleve, to Riddon and Codac.

ELLIE

Lugent? You've seen giants?

FENIAN

(*Nodding.*) Yes. And mercenaries and mages and…

ANNA

I have seen these people too. Were you frightened by the size of the Lugent Giants? I admit that I was at first.

FENIAN

A little, yes. They are abrasive when they speak, but not as coarse as speaking with Dwarves.

ELLIE

Dwarves, too?

ANNA

So, you have also been to Lafore?

FENIAN

Yes. They had just battled with the Goblins and we were brought in to help revive some of the fallen.

ELLIE

So Lady Sisk *can* bring people back?

FENIAN

I'm sorry, I have said too much...

ELLIE

It's fine. We are friends here. Please just let me know if the Queen can come back if she is taken from us.

FENIAN

(*After a pause.*) Yes…

ELLIE

Thank the Three!

ANNA

Unbelievable. I have never…

FENIAN

But it won't be her.

ELLIE

What do you mean?

FENIAN

Lady Sisk can bring back the lifeless, but they aren't the same. They become shells for stronger spirits to inhabit. Sometimes, spirits reject the body and the undead become an empty husk never to be filled. I once saw her bring back a farmer from the village where we live. He had been gone for two days before they brought the corpse to us. After hours of work, I watched him open his eyes and sit up. Seconds later, the farmer began to violently thrash about Lady Sisk's lab and even cut his wife on the arm. Then he stopped abruptly. It was as if something had left his body. He just stood there staring at the wall with his mouth open. He was rejected. The family tried to feed it and even tried to make it remember who it was, but with no success. Just a lifeless mannequin that breathed and drooled.

ELLIE

That sounds terrifying.

ANNA

And kind of gross…

FENIAN

Necromancy is no comfort.

ANNA

What happens to the bodies that the spirits accept?

FENIAN

The memories of the host and the memories of the spirit fight for control. It's violent. Watching animals go through the process is heart wrenching. Watching humans is dangerous.

ELLIE

What happened to the farmer? From your story? What did they end up doing with the body?

FENIAN

They buried it. *(Pause.)* While it was still breathing.

ANNA

Well, that was an uplifting tale.

ELLIE

I wouldn't want the Queen to go through such a terrible ordeal.

FENIAN

She won't. I'll make sure of that.

ELLIE

Thank you, Fenian.

ANNA

So I'm getting a sense that you two already got to know one another?

ELLIE

A bit, yes. I actually think our meeting was planned.

FENIAN

Oh?

ELLIE

I was told that there would be an apprentice I was to get to know better. That he would be a suitor?

ANNA

This just got more interesting.

FENIAN

Really? You knew I was coming? You knew I was going to try and—

*(Enter the **MAGISTRATE**.)*

MAGISTRATE

I do hope these two aren't troubling you, Lady Elisven?

ELLIE

Not at all, Magistrate. In fact they were regaling me with tales of their travels.

MAGISTRATE

Very good, then. I saw that Sir Ademar was approaching the castle. I was hoping to catch him as he entered.

ELLIE

He has not made his way in here yet, I am afraid.

MAGISTRATE

Knowing him, he may well have come in the service entrance at the back of the castle.

ELLIE

Most likely, yes. He is known to be humble.

MAGISTRATE

I hear his squire has taken a liking to you.

ELLIE

Squire?

MAGISTRATE

Yes. It is one of the reasons the Queen asked him to be at this meeting.

ELLIE

Oh. I had not thought about his- I blush, sir.

MAGISTRATE

He was trained in Codac, you know.

ELLIE

So I have heard.

MAGISTRATE

Maybe I could arrange for you two to…

ELLIE

I'm sure there is a better place and time to discuss this arrangement, Magistrate?

MAGISTRATE

Of course. My apologies. I will go and see if Sir Ademar has entered the castle elsewhere. (*He exits.*)

ANNA

That was embarrassing.

ELLIE

The nerve of that weasel discussing my love life in front of you two. I am sorry, Fenian. I did not realize that his squire was to be here or that he was the one the Queen wanted me to get to know.

ANNA

It must be nice to have suitors.

ELLIE

I really wouldn't know. All of this has come to light within the last few weeks.

ANNA

(Sarcastic.) No one has come to sweep the princess off her feet?

ELLIE

(*Stealing a glance at* **FENIAN**.) Not yet. The queen has insisted that I marry soon, though. Hoping to keep a crown on the throne rather than have rule fall to the council and the Magistrate.

FENIAN

That would be awful.

ELLIE

Which part? The marriage or the loss of power?

FENIAN

Maybe both. I mean, to marry without love would be terrible, but the council's rule would be a terrible thing for all of Paydunor.

ELLIE

(*Changing the subject*.) What about you, Anna? Have you ever been in love?

ANNA

Not at all. If we stayed in one place long enough, I would hope to be pursued and romanced. Instead, I just meet a few people in each town and… well… I try to keep it private. At least you'll be presented with choices.

ELLIE

Don't envy me or my situation. The whole of Paydunor knows of my love life.

ANNA

Or lack thereof?

ELLIE

Exactly. If I were to marry, then New Trale may stay under a royal rule. If I don't… If the Queen dies… The Magistrate will get to rule with his council.

ANNA

And we can't have that.

ELLIE

No, we can't. Though the Queen has turned to the council for guidance, the Queen's love for all of Paydunor's people is what keeps New Trale at peace. If the Magistrate gets his way, mages will be hunted, Poneleve will go silent and…

*(**WREN** steps out of the shadows.)*

WREN

It would be worse than you say.

(The others are startled as the demon enters the scene.)

ANNA

How long have you been there?

WREN

Long enough.

ELLIE

And you have insight into the situation I have described?

WREN

Yes.

FENIAN

You are a demon? From Poneleve?

WREN

Originally from the Gray Mountains, yes, but I have not been with demons for many years. I have lived with my master, Tofol.

ELLIE

The collector of Antiquities, yes.

ANNA

And a blue mage.

FENIAN

A mage?

WREN

It is true, yes. Tofol is powerful in the art of blue magic. He can control ice and water. He is great in years and he has collected many books and ancient items. He keeps his power hidden for he knows of a great prejudice that is on the rise against the mages.

ELLIE

He is indeed a wise man to keep his powers hidden.

WREN

He is here to try and save your Queen. He has brought an amulet that should hold off death for years to come.

ANNA

An emerald amulet with a silver chain?

WREN

Yes, of course the apprentice of a green mage would know of such an item.

ELLIE

(*Astounded.*) Ferra is a mage?

ANNA

I thought that was rather obvious.

ELLIE

Not to me.

ANNA

(*Back to **WREN**.*) And the amulet's clasp will vanish when worn?

WREN

That is it, yes. It is a treasure few books have been written about.

ANNA

My master, Lady Ferra, has been searching for that necklace ever since I have met her.

WREN

Has she?

ANNA

She claims it to be her original rune.

FENIAN

Rune?

ANNA

All mages use runes to help focus their power and energy. It becomes a part of them. They can imprint themselves into the stone and use it to learn abilities and skills.

WREN

You study your master well. You seem to know quite a lot about the life of mages.

ANNA

I do.

FENIAN

Because she is a mage herself.

ELLIE

(Shocked.) Fenian, how would you know that?

FENIAN

She has no bruises or scrapes, yet her mistress said they were attacked and handled the fight themselves.

ANNA

That doesn't mean…

FENIAN

And around her neck, look. A red stone on a silver

chain with no clasp.

ELLIE

Anna, are you a mage? Does Fenian speak the truth?

ANNA

I guess I've been found out.

ELLIE

I have never met a mage before.

ANNA

If Lady Ferra's amulet is here it may be your queen's only salvation, but my mistress will want to claim it as her own. She has always told me that her rune would call to her to return to the Marble Castle.

WREN

So that means your mistress is indeed the green mage they speak of? The amulet is not her rune, but one she created.

ANNA

Yes, a healer. I have known her to make many healing amulets.

WREN

Not just a healer.

FENIAN

Green mages are known to produce great destruction. I have heard tales of single green mages crushing entire villages with a simple whisper to the earth.

ELLIE

But she is here to heal, correct?

ANNA

That is why we are all here, but now that I know her rune is here, I have to let her know, too. *(She starts to leave.)*

WREN

Please, do not tell her. My master would be angry with me if he knew that I told.

ANNA

So why bring it up, demon?

WREN

I was seeking to know the true intentions of the Necromancer. My master feared she had come to take the amulet.

FENIAN

Lady Sisk has never mentioned an amulet or a necklace or a rune.

ANNA

Will you keep her from this knowledge? Don't let her know it is here. Please, Fenian.

ELLIE

That rune would be the answer to the Queen's needs, would it not?

FENIAN

I suppose, but...

ANNA

And she has been unsuccessful in reviving humans, if I am understanding you correctly?

FENIAN

Not unsuccessful, but her results yield an undesired...

WREN

She is here for the amulet! She has kept you in the dark!

FENIAN

I doubt that is the reason we...

ELLIE

(Getting upset. Out of character.) That *is* why you are here? To seduce me? To steal an artifact?

FENIAN

No... I was told to get to know you...

ANNA

(*Growing angry as well.*) It belongs to Ferra. (*Her hands light up in flames.*) Do not tell her of its presence here.

FENIAN

I don't understand why you are all acting this way...

(*In a flourish,* **WREN** *charges after* **FENIAN,** *but before he can attack,* **LORASON** *steps in and brandishes his sword. The demon falls back and scurries into a shadow.* **ANNA** *collapses as if being released from the grip of an unseen force.* **ELLIE** *sees this and then also collapses.*)

LORASON

A demon here in the great Marble Castle? I must warn the sentries at once. (*He starts to leave, but notices* **ELLIE** *and* **ANNA**. *He stops and helps* **ELLIE** *up.* **FENIAN** *helps* **ANNA** *to her feet hesitantly.*)

ANNA

I feel light headed.

ELLIE

Me, too.

LORASON

That creature is a manipulator. He had a hold on your minds and was feeding you unnatural thoughts.

FENIAN

Thank you for stepping in and helping us. Your name?

LORASON

Lorason, Squire to Sir Ademar.

FENIAN

Thank you, Lorason. That beast may have clawed my eyes out had you not shown up.

LORASON

No trouble. Happy to help. I was just passing through to find my knight's chambers.

ELLIE

He is known to stay with the soldiers in the barracks, correct? Those are located on the floor below here.

LORASON

Very well, then. (*He starts to leave.*)

ANNA

Don't go just yet. I think it would be good if we all got to know each other a little better, don't you?

LORASON

Okay… why, exactly?

ANNA

How often do the apprentices of a mage, a necromancer and a knight get together to discuss life?

ELLIE

Never, I imagine.

ANNA

All the more reason to stay here with us. Unless you would prefer to get in trouble with your master?

LORASON

I believe he would actually be angry at me for not staying and getting to know Lady Elisven a bit better.

ANNA

So you, too, were given the charge of winning her hand.

LORASON

Yes. It would be an honor to try and woo you, Lady Elisven.

ANNA

Very direct. I like it.

ELLIE

I am flattered. Please, tell us about yourself.

LORASON

I am but a squire to a knight. Sir Ademar is the man of legend. I have only been at his side for a year now, but everything they say about him is true. I have watched him fight Clawdashes with his sword sheathed. I have scaled the Red and Blue Mountains with him and tracked down wanted thieves and wayward Goblins. I have even seen the underground city of the Arars and have watched him discuss peace treaties with the Dwarves. I aspire to be him, Lady Elisven. If I were to continue my training, were I to be half the man he is, I am certain I could make you proud and happy as a husband.

ANNA

That was brought up fast.

ELLIE

I think it best we get to know one another better, Lorason.

LORASON

Why? My charge was to win your hand in marriage. We have a lifetime to learn about one another. Let us save Paydunor by joining each other's lives in the eyes of the Three.

ELLIE

Surely this has not just become a marriage proposal?

LORASON

I admit to being wary of what my knight had asked of me regarding you, but after seeing you, your beauty, I know now that I was a fool to doubt my master's intentions. Let me help you save the crown, Lady Elisven.

ELLIE

This is happening awfully fast.

ANNA

I'll say.

ELLIE

I just learned your name a moment ago.

LORASON

The stories and songs of old are about lovers that move just as quickly. They will write songs of us one day.

FENIAN

I think she would like to get to know you better before making a rushed decision in the moment.

LORASON

And who are you? A lowborn, poor and unkempt pile of street trash!

ELLIE

That is uncalled for, Lorason.

LORASON

Is he not my rival for your hand?

*(**ELLIE** and **FENIAN** look at each other.)*

ANNA

He is. What of it?

ELLIE

*(Talking to **ANNA**, so the boys don't hear.)* What are you doing, Anna?

ANNA

Haven't you ever wanted to have two men fight over you?

ELLIE

No.

ANNA

Well, I have and now I can live secondhand through you.

LORASON

Are you willing to fight for her, sir?

ELLIE

Fenian, you don't have to do this.

ANNA

Yes, he does. (*To **ELLIE**.*) Don't ruin this for me.

FENIAN

Okay.

ELLIE

What?

FENIAN

I'll do it. I'll fight.

ELLIE

He is a trained squire, Fenian.

FENIAN

If he defeats me, your choice will be easier.

ELLIE

This is not the way I want to choose a husband.

LORASON

And yet, we have still decided to fight for you, my lady. (*He draws his sword.*)

ELLIE

This is too much! This is not what I wanted!

QUEEN

(*Entering.*) It wasn't what I expected for you either.

LORASON

Your Majesty.

(*They all kneel.*)

I was wanting to prove myself to your ward.

QUEEN

And in the process, stain my marble floors with blood?

LORASON

I am sorry, Your Grace. I was angry. I should have

calmed down and walked away, but from the moment I saw your ward, I fell madly in love with her. I will fight for her hand in marriage.

QUEEN

And you, boy?

FENIAN

Your Majesty?

QUEEN

Who do you belong to?

FENIAN

Lady Sisk, your grace.

QUEEN

I see. I think it would be best if you all stand out of the way. My guests will be arriving for the meeting here soon. Come Ellie. Sit by me.

*(Two guards enter and place two ornate chairs for the **QUEEN** and **ELLIE** to sit. The Queen pulls on a gold rope that rings a summoning bell. The others on stage move apart ashamed of their actions.)*

My dear, tell me what happened here.

ELLIE

It happened so fast, the demon was here, then Lorason showed up and before we were finished thanking him for running the little beast off, he was ready to fight and attack Fenian.

QUEEN

The one you actually like?

ELLIE

I got to know him better. He seems kind, but broken.

QUEEN

Broken men can be hard to fix, my dear.

ELLIE

So I should choose the squire?

QUEEN

I merely presented you with the opportunity to meet the squire. If neither of them make you feel any different, then neither of them are the one. We will keep looking for your king.

(TOFOL, WREN, Sir ADEMAR, FERRA and Lady SISK enter from various locations as the apprentices move to stand by their masters. The MAGISTRATE walks in and stands by the Queen. All bow as the QUEEN stands.)

My time is short. You have been called here to help me in my time of need. I believe that what is best for New Trale, for Paydunor and for the people, is that the crown stays in the ruling power. I ask that you, my guests, rejuvenate my life or find a way to bring me back after death.

(She sits.)

The floor is yours. Speak freely.

SISK

My queen, I would like to… *(As the scene continues to play out, SISK tries to speak over the group.)*

ADEMAR

My queen, in my travels I have learned, from many people, that death can be avoided with the right magic and herbs. Allow me to travel to Lafore and Lugent. I could bring you the Silks of the Arar, a draught that is known to restore youth.

QUEEN

I'm afraid there is no time for travel.

TOFOL

After examining our Queen, I have found that, in her state, it may be within the week that death will take her.

QUEEN

Lady Ferra, do you have a proposed solution?

FERRA

To cheat death? No. Perhaps if your malady was of a physical nature I could heal you.

ADEMAR

You doubt what her Grace has said to us? You doubt she is sick?

FERRA

She is sick, Ademar, but no physical ailment is affecting her.

ADEMAR

How dare you accuse our sovereign of not having the mental…

QUEEN

Let her speak, Sir Ademar.

FERRA

I have heard Tofol's diagnosis, but I am unconvinced. I feel as though your sickness is that of the mind. You have seen hardship. You have watched this world tear itself apart and mend back together. Your Highness, you have seen prejudice rise within your own court while fighting atrocities in the north and east. The mind can only handle so much darkness before it turns to the body for help.

TOFOL

So then you see this as a psychosis?

MAGISTRATE

Were this the case, Lady Ferra, her majesty would be unfit to rule. I would move to have the council take…

FERRA

There is a solution.

ADEMAR

There is no cure for damaged minds.

FERRA

Rest, Your Grace.

MAGISTRATE

Rest? Your solution is for the crown to nap?

FERRA

And eat. I suggest she goes away from here. Away from the pressures of ruling.

TOFOL

And leave the throne empty? For how long?

FERRA

As long as it takes.

TOFOL

That could be weeks; months even!

FERRA

It is my suggestion.

ADEMAR

I could keep her safe on this journey. Where should we take her?

TOFOL

Now see here, I am not convinced this is all in her mind. There are traces of illness. There are symptoms that are recorded in books that she has shown.

FERRA

Then what is your suggestion, Tofol? What is your remedy?

TOFOL

I would rather discuss that in private, Lady Ferra.

FERRA

Have you?

QUEEN

He has.

FERRA

Then why have the pretense of this meeting?

QUEEN

Tofol came to me. You could have done the same.

MAGISTRATE

I think we should all hear what Tofol's remedy is. Let it be public.

FERRA

I have to agree with the Magistrate, Tofol.

(Pause.)

TOFOL

We have yet to hear from Lady Sisk.

SISK

(Annoyed.) Do I get to speak now?

QUEEN

If it please you, Lady Sisk. What could a necromancer do for me?

SISK

My queen. Let me start by thanking you for the lovely invitation and the chance to see…

ADEMAR

On with it, witch!

SISK

Very well. I have had successes bringing the dead back into the world of the living. I have had failures too. It is not a pretty process and can have unnatural results. Everything we need is here, in this hall, in those satchels and in the hearts of those standing here. To bring a life back, a life must be freely given to the deceased. Any of your loyal servants, I'm sure, are willing to give their lives for you. But before any volunteers come forward, let me say this: the more powerful the mind of the sacrifice, the more likely we will have success. I suggest that we use the life of someone in this room. The greatest minds of Paydunor are here. They are at your disposal.

TOFOL

This is preposterous! She is a fake. All recorded acts of necromancy were either failures or hoaxes.

FERRA

I have never seen a necromancy spell as a success.

ADEMAR

Most of Paydunor looks down on the dark art of life reanimation.

SISK

Do you say this because you are unwilling to give your life for your queen or do you truly doubt my skills?

QUEEN

For you to use your talents, Lady Sisk, I would have to first die?

SISK

Yes, Your Grace. Let me stay here and be your last hope. These others may have remedies, but I can bring you back after the unthinkable has occurred.

FERRA

We are trying to give her longevity, not…

SISK

When I am successful, the life after her return she will be eternal!

(Pause.)

QUEEN

Eternal? Life everlasting…

SISK

Yes, my Queen. When I bring one back from the shadows it is no longer needed to leave the living again. The life is dead, the soul gone, but the mind and body can continue.

TOFOL

This is lunacy, Your Majesty. Do not give this street performer any merit.

FERRA

Then share with us, Tofol, your thoughts and answers.

ELLIE

My Queen, please, do not let the necromancer practice her art. Her apprentice has told me stories. Ghastly tales of what could happen to you.

SISK

(*Indignant.*) He did? Fenian, what did you tell the queen's ward?

QUEEN

Step forward, apprentice.

(***FENIAN*** *moves to the center of the hall. Everyone gives him the floor.*)

SISK

(*To **FENIAN**.*) You best think about what you say to her in these next moments. (*Addressing the **QUEEN**.*) I'm sure he told the Lady Elisven of our successes as well as the darker tales.

QUEEN

Fenian is your name?

FENIAN

Yes, m' Lady- Your Majesty.

QUEEN

Tell me the dark tale that you told Lady Elisven, please.

FENIAN

I don't think I was truly able to tell her what…

ELLIE

The farmer, Fenian. Tell her of the farmer and what became of him.

FENIAN

I… I am not sure if I can or…

ELLIE

He was just a shell of a man. A brain-dead husk that breathed. A mannequin of flesh and bone. She brought him back to life, but there was no life to the living body.

SISK

*(To **FENIAN**.)* You stupid, insolent, fool of a boy. I should have you beaten.

QUEEN

No! Fenian, speak. What had become of the farmer?

FENIAN

We buried him, Your Majesty.

QUEEN

Was his life eternal, Lady Sisk?

SISK

I… I'm not sure if…

QUEEN

Did you bury a man alive that will live out eternity under the soil?

SISK

…yes, your majesty.

(Pause.)

QUEEN

Take her away. *(Guards enter and grab **SISK**.)* Put her in a lower room and lock the door. I will think on how to punish such a despicable deed at the conclusion of this meeting.

SISK

Your majesty, no! Please I can save you! I can help you!

QUEEN

Take her from my sight now!

*(The guards drag **SISK** away as she screams from off stage.)*

SISK

Fenian! Fenian! You will pay with your life for ruining me, Fenian! I will see you back on the streets or dead in a ditch! I swear it! By the Three I swear it!

(SISK has exited with the guards as the QUEEN stands again. All bow.)

QUEEN

I have heard your advice. I will heed all of your counsel, but I hope to think on it by myself in my chambers. Ferra, your recommendation for rest, is one I hope to take. Tofol, your gift is one I want to examine soon in the library. Ademar, thank you for your concern. I know I can trust you to be by my side should I choose to journey away from my kingdom. Now I must go and rest. Magistrate, please make sure our guests are seen to.

ELLIE

Shall I take you to your room, my queen?

QUEEN

No, thank you, my dear. Please see to the others. Make sure we find a place for Fenian.

ELLIE

Yes, your grace.

(The QUEEN exits.)

MAGISTRATE

Lady Ferra, Sir Ademar, let me show you to your chambers. This way please.

TOFOL

Wren and I will take our leave as well.

FERRA

We will speak soon, Tofol.

TOFOL

I am sure we will.

(TOFOL and WREN exit.)

FERRA

Come Anna. Let us prepare for the Queen's journey.

ANNA

If I may be so bold to ask, Lady Ferra, I would like to stay with the Lady Elisven and the other apprentices.

FERRA

Very well. Find me after dark.

ANNA

Of course, my Lady.

ADEMAR

(*To* **FERRA**.) Might I accompany you, my Lady? I wish to also discuss arrangements for the Queen's departure.

FERRA

It would be my pleasure.

(*FERRA,* **ADEMAR** *and the* **MAGISTRATE** *exit.)*

ELLIE

I am so sorry Fenian. I had no idea she would be taken to the dungeons below.

ANNA

You have to admit it was a fitting punishment.

ELLIE

No jokes, Anna, please. Can't you see Fenian is distraught?

ANNA

I am sorry, truly I am, but what she did was terrible and inhuman. Serves her right to be locked away down there.

ELLIE

What will you do Fenian?

FENIAN

I… I have nothing else…

ELLIE

Oh, Fenian. (*She hugs him*.) Maybe I can find a way to keep you here. Maybe you can work for the castle stewards or in the library.

LORASON

Ridiculous. If you keep him around, he will just let the dark witch out one night and the two of them will get their revenge on the entire castle.

ELLIE

I don't think that would be the case.

LORASON

He wouldn't be the mind behind it, but Sisk is dangerous... If she is telling the truth. If he is telling the truth...

FENIAN

I wasn't lying about what I said. I saw what I saw.

LORASON

If she isn't a fraud then she is dangerous! He is dangerous!

ELLIE

You have said enough!

LORASON

Not enough, obviously, since she is still here and he isn't being punished for playing a part in her misdeeds.

ELLIE

Fenian had nothing to do with the atrocities that night with the farmer, did you?

FENIAN

I was there. I helped.

LORASON

You see?! He admits to being a part of it! He admits to helping and learning from his master necromancer.

ANNA

Of course he does. That's what we do. We are apprentices. We learn a trade. Most of the time it isn't even our choice in where we...

LORASON

So we should let the trade of dark magic continue? We should let him run loose and teach others how to unnaturally bring back the dead, turning them into nothing more than walking flesh!?

ELLIE

You are getting heated over a topic that has nothing to do with you!

LORASON

It does! I am to be the one to end the line of necromancers. (*He draws his sword.*) Face me! If they won't write songs of our love, Lady Elisven, they will write songs of vicotory!

ELLIE

Anna, quick go get the guards.

(***ANNA*** *runs out of the hall.*)

LORASON

Face me! Coward! (*He strikes* ***FENIAN*** *who falls to the ground.*)

ELLIE

Lorason, no!

LORASON

Get up! Face me!

ELLIE

That is enough, Lorason. I command you to stop!

(***LORASON*** *strikes* ***FENIAN*** *again.* ***FENIAN*** *turns as* ***LORASON*** *stands over him.* ***LORASON*** *raises his sword above his head.* ***ELLIE*** *runs over and tackles* ***LORASON*** *to the ground.* ***LORASON*** *stands up and slaps* ***ELLIE***. ***ELLIE*** *falls.* ***FENIAN*** *stands up as* ***LORASON*** *rushes towards him, sword in hand.* ***FENIAN*** *stretches out his hands. There is a bright flash and fog.* ***FENIAN'S*** *hands are blue, spikes of ice protrude from* ***LORASON***. *The squire falls to the ground.* ***WREN*** *steps out of the shadows.*)

Curtain

Act II

*(**FENIAN** is kneeling on one side of the stage. **LORASON**'s lifeless body is center stage, spikes of ice still protruding from his body. **ELLIE** still stands shocked at what has happened. **WREN** begins to exit quietly but is seen by **ELLIE**.)*

ELLIE

Stop, you monster!

*(**ELLIE** runs and grabs **WREN**.)*

Did you do this? Did you manipulate us into killing him?

WREN

You were merely defending yourselves-

ELLIE

You had nothing to do with this? You didn't make Lorason attack Fenian?

WREN

I planted the desire, but-

ELLIE

*(Releasing **WREN** and rushing over to **FENIAN**)* What do we do? I have never seen a dead- I have never known someone to… What did you do, Fenian?

FENIAN

I don't know, Ellie. I just held up my hands… and then… ice…

WREN

He is a blue mage. My master can do the same as you have demonstrated.

*(**FENIAN** stands and rushes over to **WREN**.)*

Do not hurt me, please. I was trying to know your true intentions. I meant for no one to get harmed.

FENIAN

It is because of you that someone is dead. This is on your head. You made him angry. You made me attack.

WREN

I made him angry, yes. I can stir emotions. It was you who shot the ice, young mage. It was you who ended a life. I did nothing to move you to attack.

ELLIE

There is no sense in debating with this demon.

FENIAN

We have to tell someone. Ademar? The Queen?

(Pause.)

ELLIE

No.

FENIAN

No?

ELLIE

If the Magistrate finds out that you are a mage, you will not be safe. You will be hunted by his appointed guard. You may not even make it out of the city, Fenian. With Lady Sisk in the dungeons below, you would be scrutinized. You would be blamed for his death and it would be twisted to look like an act of vengeance. I don't want anything to happen to you.

FENIAN

What do you suggest we do?

WREN

You could hide the body, young mage.

*(**FENIAN** starts towards **WREN** with intent to hit.)*

Stop, please. Let me help. Let me make amends. I am one who knows things about blue mages. I am one who can help you.

FENIAN

(*To* **ELLIE**.) Does the Queen know Tofol and Ferra are mages?

ELLIE

Not to my knowledge.

FENIAN

(*To* **WREN**.) What is the artifact that Tofol has that he wants to give the Queen?

WREN

As the others have said, it is a green rune with healing powers. It can block death… or so the legends say. It has never been used that I know of.

FENIAN

Get me that rune to make up for your atrocities.

WREN

I cannot steal from my master. You ask too much of me. I am a loyal servant. I act on the will of Tofol.

FENIAN

Did Tofol make you do this? Did he want you to manipulate us? Turn us against one another?

WREN

I have said too much. Please don't say anything to my master, please.

ELLIE

Help us hide the body.

WREN

Then you will leave me alone? We will be even?

FENIAN

Far from it.

ELLIE

You are the one who actively mistreated us! It is you who will need to leave us out of your master's plans. Now help us move Lorason.

FENIAN

Wait. I think I can bring him back.

ELLIE

What are you saying?

FENIAN

He hasn't been dead long. His spirit may still be strong enough or close enough... I don't really understand the logistics of it... but I think I can bring him back and with the rune that Tofol has, maybe we can keep him sustained.

WREN

I said I would not help you get my master's...

ELLIE

(*To* **WREN**.) Quiet, beast! (*To* **FENIAN**.) Are you sure you can do this? Are you sure you *want* to do this? Don't we need another...

FENIAN

I can and I do want to do this. We need to hide the body and I will need to find a way to get supplies.

ELLIE

Then we will need to get close to Tofol and steal the rune.

WREN

No! I won't let you-

(**ELLIE** *punches* **WREN** *in the face. He drops down stunned*)

I didn't desire that violence.

ELLIE

You did. Not with any manipulation, but by speaking. Now get up and help us.

(**WREN** *gets to his feet and grabs the arms of* **LORISON** *and drags him off stage.* **ELLIE** *follows but stops short of exiting and looks back at* **FENIAN**.)

I know where we can keep the body hidden until we

have what we need.

FENIAN

You punched the little fiend.

ELLIE

I did, yeah…

FENIAN

Lady Elisven, the Demon Puncher.

ELLIE

Come on, no time for jokes. Let's hide Lorason.

FENIAN

I'll be right there. (*He watches* **ELLIE** *exit before looking up to recite a prayer.*)

A sun that rises

A moon that will set

A moon that looks on

For us they have wept.

We pray to you

The sisters three

Please bless us now

Answer our plea

With Life and Death

and Antiquity.

(*FENIAN grabs the satchels and bags from the stage and exits. After a moment, ANNA enters with FERRA and TOFOL.*)

ANNA

They were in here. Lorason was out of control ready to kill Fenian. His sword was drawn and he was ranting and raving. It was like he went crazy. It was brought on so quickly, like his inner demons were triggered.

FERRA

I doubt there was anything inner about his demons,

Anna.

TOFOL

Is that an accusation towards my assistant, Lady Ferra? I can assure you, Wren is no monster like the mindless drones in Poneleve.

FERRA

Over strong willed minds like yours and mine, I am sure he is powerless. But these are teenaged minds. They are still children who have not yet lived to see two decades pass. Their wills have not been trained. We have had lifetimes dealing with dark creatures.

TOFOL

Well, I am certain of Wren's capabilities.

FERRA

Anna, where are our fighters? The hall is empty.

ANNA

I don't know. I left them here only moments ago. I don't know where they could have gone.

TOFOL

Perhaps Ademar intervened?

FERRA

He had just left my company when you came to find me. Did he not pass you in the corridor?

ANNA

Should I go back to find him, Lady Ferra?

FERRA

Yes. That may be best. Tofol and I will stay here in case the fighting youths return.

ANNA

Yes, m'Lady. (*She exits.*)

(*Pause.*)

FERRA

Do you know where Wren is at this moment, Tofol?

TOFOL

In the chambers we were given, I'm sure.

FERRA

You do not seem very confident.

TOFOL

Do not try and implicate my demon in this mess.

FERRA

Anna said that she felt manipulated. She described it as a force that had a grip on her mind and was filling her with rage. That sounds familiar, does it not?

TOFOL

We don't even know if anything has happened. Children fight. Adults fight. This could just be a misunderstanding as the two boys quarrel for Lady Elisven's hand in marriage. Let us change the subject until they show again.

FERRA

We are the only ones here.

TOFOL

Yes. What of it?

FERRA

Let us stop all pretenses, blue mage. You know why I answered the Queen's summons and risked my life to be under the same roof as the Magistrate. Let us discuss the item you have that I want back, shall we?

TOFOL

Ferra, you gave me that amulet hundreds of years ago…

FERRA

With the intention that if it served you and the unfortunate still befell her, you would return it. It is a part of me Tofol.

TOFOL

It is a part of her, too! And a part of me…

FERRA

It is my life force, my energy that keeps it active. That keeps it healing the wearer. Let me have it back. Let me feel a bit more whole. Too often in my youth I gave parts of me away to heal the unfortunate. I now have to track down those pieces, Tofol.

TOFOL

It's all I have left of her…

FERRA

Maybe it is time you let her go completely. How many years has it been since she passed?

TOFOL

I don't remember. A century? Maybe more. I… It wasn't long after she left this plane that Wren came to my door. He was the distraction I needed. I used my time with him to learn anatomy. Trying to see if there was something I missed. Something physical I could have done to keep her here with me.

FERRA

She was human, Tofol. A temporary creature that was taken to the Three.

TOFOL

I still feel her in the amulet, though, Ferra. As if her essence is in there. I feel you, too, when the amulet is in use. You would have liked her, I think.

FERRA

My fondness for the humans is diminishing with each passing year.

TOFOL

Are we not humans with gifts? Do you want us to claim ourselves as a different race? The Magistrate knows you are a mage, doesn't he?

FERRA

Yes. His men attacked us as we journeyed here. He has a plot and a hand he has not played yet, but it is one that will present itself soon. These are dangerous times for our kind.

TOFOL

Indeed. (*Pause.*) I was to give it to the Queen. Your amulet. She is deciding if she will use it or not.

FERRA

Why give it to the Queen and not return it to me?

TOFOL

Honestly? The Queen looks like her. I don't think I could live with myself if I did nothing as she slowly dies.

FERRA

Nothing will stop the Magistrate from seizing power. But you might be able to delay it with that amulet hanging around the Queen's neck. We shall see.

*(Enter **ANNA** and **ADEMAR**.)*

My apprentice returns.

ANNA

Yes, Lady Ferra. I have the knight as you requested.

ADEMAR

I hear my squire and the necromancer's boy were fighting.

FERRA

That is the rumor, but we have yet to see either of them, Sir Ademar.

ADEMAR

If it is true, my squire will be disciplined, that I can assure you.

TOFOL

There is no doubt in my mind that this is all just one big misunderstanding.

ANNA

It looked to me that they both understood exactly what they were doing.

FERRA

(*Sharply.*) Hush, Anna.

ANNA

Apologies, Lady Ferra.

ADEMAR

You don't know where they went?

ANNA

No, sir.

ADEMAR

Perhaps I should conduct a thorough search of the castle's southern rooms.

TOFOL

An apt plan, Sir Knight.

ADEMAR

I do hope your demon is not behind any of these violent actions, old man. I have slain many of the scaled beasts for lesser offenses.

TOFOL

I can assure you, he is not to blame in this matter. Now I will return to my room and my demon assistant, and continue my research. (He exits.)

ADEMAR

I am taking my leave to the southern rooms.

FERRA

Ademar, a moment please?

ADEMAR

Yes, my Lady?

FERRA

If you find them in mid-brawl, please keep in mind they are just boys. They are thinking with clouded minds while around the Queen's ward.

ADEMAR

I will keep that in mind, my Lady. (He exits.)

FERRA

It is just us now, Anna. Tell me more about what happened.

ANNA

I could feel the demon inside my mind, Ferra. He kept making me urge the two to fight. I couldn't fight my own thoughts, because they were my thoughts. It was what I wanted. I would have never said anything out loud had it not been for that demon.

FERRA

I understand, Anna. At least you are safe.

ANNA

What are you going to do? Were you able to convince Tofol to give you the amulet?

FERRA

On the contrary, I have given up on the amulet. The old mage led me to a realization I had not thought of. (*FERRA senses something in the air. She investigates the floor where LORASON had fallen.*) Strange… Tofol was not in the room when the two boys were fighting?

ANNA

No, my Lady.

FERRA

(*To herself.*) So I was right. Just wrong about the outcome.

ANNA

My Lady?

FERRA

Nothing. I am sorry, Anna. I was just musing aloud. I think I will go downstairs and speak with the captive Necromancer.

ANNA

Shall I accompany you?

FERRA

That will not be necessary. Stay here until our

trio of young lovers return. (She Exits.)

*(After a beat, **ELLIE** walks onstage looking behind herself.)*

ANNA

There you are!

ELLIE

Shhh! Fenian is still hiding him.

ANNA

Hiding him? Hiding who? (*Realizing what she might have missed*.) Oh no… How was Fenian able to…

ELLIE

You have to promise not to tell anyone.

ANNA

You have my word.

ELLIE

Fenian is a blue mage.

ANNA

A MAGE!

ELLIE

Shhh!

ANNA

I'm sorry. A mage? How do you know? Did he… (*She starts waving her hand in a spastic fashion.*)

ELLIE

Yes. Ice shot from his palms and into Lorason.

ANNA

I didn't think the little man had it in him.

ELLIE

It was the demon, Wren, controlling them. He admitted to it.

ANNA

So that should free Fenian of any guilt.

ELLIE

Not with the Magistrate out for mage blood. We need to keep his powers hidden.

ANNA

Okay. So where is Fenian now?

ELLIE

He is hiding the body by the southern kitchen. Hoping the heat will melt the weapon.

ANNA

It sounds like self-defense.

ELLIE

It was. We hope the ice will melt and then we can stage his death as an accident somehow.

ANNA

Now that sounds a bit more underhanded than I anticipated from you, princess.

ELLIE

I am no princess.

ANNA

Wait. Did you say southern kitchen?

ELLIE

Yes, why?

ANNA

This just got real bad real fast.

ELLIE

What is it, Anna?

ANNA

Ademar is searching the Southern rooms for Lorason and Fenian.

ELLIE

We have to warn him! (*She starts to exit.*)

ANNA

Ellie, wait!

ELLIE

Why wait? We have to get him away from the body or Lorason will know that he had something to do with his death.

ANNA

It's most likely too late.

(*There is a crash from off stage.* **WREN** *runs onstage and is chased by* **FENIAN**.)

FENIAN

Stop him! Quick! Before he gets away.

(**WREN** *is too quick for* **ANNA** *and just barely misses* **ELLIE** *grabbing him.* **WREN** *runs offstage.* **FENIAN** *collapses. He is exhausted.*)

We dragged him to the kitchens and then overheard servants talking of Ademar who is in the corridor looking for Lorason. (*Standing surprised to see* **ANNA**.) Oh Anna! I…

ELLIE

It's okay. She knows.

FENIAN

How much does she know? Does she know I'm a…

ANNA

An Ice-Cold killer? Yes, I have been filled in on the details surrounding your little accident.

FENIAN

The more I replay the events in my mind, the less and less I think it was an accident. It was an action I somehow knew I could do. I imagined it as it happened…

ELLIE

It was self defense, Fenian. Don't think so low

of yourself. You were protecting yourself as well as protecting me.

FENIAN

I have never killed anyone before. I have never intentionally hurt anyone. I don't know what to do, Ellie.

ELLIE

We need to come up with a story that keeps you safe. That keeps you with me.

FENIAN

More lies? I don't think I can.

ANNA

And yet, Ellie is having no trouble at all. I kind of like this darker side her.

FENIAN

So what is the plan? To say he fell on a pike?

ANNA

Lorason was skipping along merrily through the marble corridor until he tripped over his own two feet and fell into the kitchen where he impaled himself on several rolling pins.

FENIAN

You may see this as a time for levity, Anna, but it isn't. I may as well go lock myself downstairs with Lady Sisk now. It will save me the embarrassment of a trial.

ELLIE

We'll think of something. I am sure of it.

ADEMAR

(Offstage.) Call the guards! Get the Queen!

ANNA

I hope you two can think fast on your feet. Ademar seems to have found Lorason.

ADEMAR

(*Entering in a rage.*) Where is the master of

antiquity? (*To* **ANNA**.) Bring me Tofol! (*Anna exits.*)

ELLIE

(*Feigning surprise.*) Why, Sir Knight?

ADEMAR

I have found my squire, Lorason, dead. His body had spikes of ice protruding from him. There is only one man in this castle that can do such a thing.

ELLIE

How could Tofol do such an evil act? Why accuse the old man?

ADEMAR

He is one of the abominations the Magistrate warns us about.

ELLIE

You mean he is a…

ADEMAR

A blue mage, yes. One capable of controlling ice and water to create destruction! To take the life from an innocent in such a horrific way… It's barbaric!

ELLIE

I am sorry to hear of Lorason's unfortunate accident.

ADEMAR

This was no accident child. This was a murder and one done maliciously- You! (*He turns his attention to* **FENIAN**.) You were fighting with him for this girl here. What did you see? What were his last words? Did you see Tofol?

FENIAN

I… I… We didn't really have a long altercation… it was…

ELLIE

It was more of a shouting match, really. Lorason left in anger when I made my choice to marry Fenian.

FENIAN

Wait, what…?

ELLIE

He was angry and ran off to the southern corridor.

ADEMAR

So you did not see the old mage?

FENIAN

I did not, no, but…

ADEMAR

Someone must have seen him attack Lorason. I will have blood for this!

(The QUEEN enters with TOFOL, ANNA and the MAGISTRATE. ADEMAR starts at TOFOL.)

You! How could you? He was just a child. He had not yet seen true combat. He was here to woo the Queen's ward. He meant no harm.

TOFOL

I say, what are you accusing me of?

QUEEN

Please, Ademar, calm yourself and speak plainly.

ADEMAR

My squire, Lorason, is dead. Killed by a mage's ice attack.

QUEEN

There are no mages here, Sir Knight.

ADEMAR

There is, my Queen. And he stands here among us. Tofol is a blue mage and a murderer.

MAGISTRATE

That is quite an accusation.

ADEMAR

Half of which I know you to believe, Magistrate.

QUEEN

Elaborate, please.

ADEMAR

The Magistrate knows of Tofol's abilities and was waiting to tell you once his suspicions were found to be true. The proof is what punctured and ended the life of my squire. His ice is still embedded in Lorason as we speak.

QUEEN

Are you a mage, Tofol?

TOFOL

Indeed, Your Majesty. I am a blue mage. I kept this from you for my own selfish protection. I am sorry for the deceit, but I am no murderer.

QUEEN

Thank you, Ademar, for bringing this to light, but I am afraid Tofol is not your killer. He was with me when these events must have transpired. He even came to me with concern for your squire after he heard the news of the fight between the two boys.

ADEMAR

If he is not the mage who killed Lorason, who is? What other mages are hiding in our midst?

MAGISTRATE

My Queen, I move to have myself and the council begin interrogating all who are suspected of being a mage immediately. (*To **ADEMAR**.*) We will smoke out this culprit and find your justice. (*To **TOFOL**.*) As for this mage here, I think it would be prudent to lock him below with Lady Sisk.

QUEEN

That will not be necessary. I feel weak. Take my hand Tofol. (***TOFOL** walks over and does as she asks.*) I think, in light of events, my time is upon me. The amulet is needed.

MAGISTRATE

My Queen, do you think it safe to trust one of them?

QUEEN

I trust him with my life.

MAGISTRATE

Do you think it wise, Your Majesty? Under the circumstances we find ourselves in, I think it best we use caution when dealing with these mages.

QUEEN

Your concern is noted. Thank you, Magistrate.

TOFOL

If you will excuse us now. (*He and the* **QUEEN** *start to exit.*)

ADEMAR

Do not think I have ruled you out as a possibility, old man. If I cannot find the blue mage responsible, I will see you hung in his stead.

QUEEN

It is impolite, Ademar, to make threats while in a sovereign's presence.

ADEMAR

My apologies. I speak out of turn while distraught. I will refrain while you are here.

QUEEN

It is best you do. Come Tofol. (*The* **QUEEN** *and* **TOFOL** *exit.*)

MAGISTRATE

And you three saw nothing?

ELLIE

No, Magistrate.

ANNA

I had left for help while they became heated. I only just learned of Lorason's death.

MAGISTRATE

And you, boy? I keep hearing of a fight.

FENIAN

(*Struggling to lie.*) We were fighting for Lady Elisven. But he left when…

ADEMAR

That seems out of character for him.

ELLIE

I thought the same thing. He acted as a mad fool and stormed off.

ADEMAR

I am going to go and stand by his side. We should be bringing the body here shortly.

MAGISTRATE

I shall join you. We have much to discuss.

(*The **MAGISTRATE** and **ADEMAR** start to exit. **FENIAN** steps forward.*)

FENIAN

I could bring him back.

(*Pause as the **MAGISTRATE** and **ADEMAR** turn around.*)

ELLIE

Fenian, wait. I have this…

FENIAN

That is… I think I can. If we could have Lady Sisk out here to observe, I am sure I could perform the necessary rituals and make the draughts needed for him to come back.

MAGISTRATE

And have the boy be cursed to be an empty shell of flesh? No. I think it best to let the young man stay at peace.

ADEMAR

The Magistrate is right. Let Lorason rest. I will have his vengeance. (*He exits with the **MAGISTRATE**.*)

ANNA

You know, if the whole queen thing doesn't work

for you, Ellie, you'd make a great actress.

ELLIE

Go find your mistress, Anna. Maybe we can confide in her.

*(**ANNA** Exits. **FENIAN** sits on the steps and **ELLIE** sits next to him. She lays her head on his shoulder.)*

I'm sorry Fenian. I know you didn't want me to lie, but I wanted to protect you.

FENIAN

I know. I'm still in disbelief that I did what I did. I don't feel any different. I mean, I feel guilty, but I don't feel like I am a mage.

ELLIE

Maybe Ferra will take you and train you.

FENIAN

She already has an apprentice. I'm sure I would just be a burden.

ELLIE

You are not a burden Fenian.

(Pause.)

You know… I meant what I said. About choosing you.

FENIAN

It was just part of your lie.

ELLIE

The best lies are told with hints of truth.

*(**ELLIE** leans in and kisses **FENIAN**.)*

FENIAN

Ellie?

ELLIE

Yeah?

FENIAN

I am so confused right now…

*(The two kiss again. They stop as **ANNA** enters with **FERRA** and **SISK**. **SISK** has her hands in shackles.)*

ANNA

I hope we weren't interrupting anything?

ELLIE

(*Standing*.) Not at all. Did you tell Lady Ferra everything- What is *she* doing here?

SISK

I heard my little Fenian had something he was hiding from me all this time.

FENIAN

I can't hide something I didn't know I had.

SISK

When we leave from here, you will have a lot of explaining to do.

FENIAN

If we leave from here. Will you help bring him back, m'Lady?

SISK

Who?

FENIAN

Lorason.

SISK

The squire boy?

FENIAN

Yes, m'Lady. I…

FERRA

So it is true.

SISK

I seem to be the only party here missing some vital details to this mystery.

FERRA

Fenian, in a rage, killed Lorason with his newly discovered gifts.

SISK

(*Stunned.*) Is this true Fenian? (***FENIAN** nods.*) I didn't think you had it in you, boy. Ha! Here I am trying to bring back the dead and you simply snap your fingers and extinguish a life. This will no doubt make it harder for me to sell my trade.

FENIAN

Lady Sisk, please. Help me bring him back.

SISK

Hush up you little executioner! I doubt the Magistrate or the knight will let me anywhere near the body. Besides, I don't think I would. Who would pay us, were we to be successful?

FENIAN

I am not an executioner. It was self defense… I don't even know how I did it. I just feel we should to make amends.

SISK

I think it would be wiser for us to leave this place far behind and go back to the Tower where I will beat you within an inch of your life!

ELLIE

There will be no beatings, Lady Sisk. I have chosen Fenian to be my husband.

SISK

(*Stunned pause.*) What?

ELLIE

And once we are wed, I will be made Queen and he will rule as…

SISK

My Fenian, as your husband? As a king? (*She laughs.*) I can't believe it. He pulled it off. (*She laughs.*) And to think, when I found you on the streets of Riddon… Who would have known that my piece of gutter-trash would one day be a ruler in Paydunor and shoot magic from his finger nails!

ELLIE

(*To* **FENIAN**.) I can't really tell if she is happy for you or…

FENIAN

I'm never sure if she is happy or angry. I think it's the same emotion for her.

SISK

Now, Lady Ferra, if you would be so kind as to undo these chains.

FERRA

What makes you think I have a way to do that?

SISK

Oh, please, let's not act innocent. Wave your hands or whatever it is you do and use the green magic to undo the restraints.

FERRA

Is the Queen really the only one who does not know I am a mage?

SISK

It would appear so. (*She raises her wrists and chains*.) Please?

FERRA

Very well. (*With a subtle flip of her wrist,* **SISK**'*s chains fall*.)

SISK

Thank you. (**SISK** *dashes to* **FENIAN** *and starts to hit him repeatedly*.) How could you not tell me you had power! We could have taken advantage of this for so long! Think of how wealthy we could be right now!

FENIAN

Stop, m'Lady, Please! (*There is another flash and fog.* **SISK** *flies back off of* **FENIAN** *and to the ground.* FINEAN's *hands are blue again*.)

SISK

You wicked little magician. How dare you strike me with your…

FERRA

His powers are reactionary, Lady Sisk. I do not think you should continue provoking him.

SISK

Let me ask you something, Lady Ferra: Why let me out? Why risk your life and reputation to save me from the Marble Castle's dungeons?

FERRA

My concern was for Fenian. When Anna brought me to this room, I knew magic had been used. I could feel the ice. I put the pieces of the story together and was hoping you would take him away from here. Keep him safe long enough so I could come to you, collect Fenian and train him.

SISK

You would want to take him away from me? You already have an apprentice.

FERRA

Anna is strong enough to venture on her own. She no longer needs me. Fenian does. I can help him channel his power. Give him control.

ANNA

She will teach him and train him well.

SISK

For a price.

FERRA

I can assure you, my service would be free for him.

SISK

No, you misunderstand. How much will you give me for the boy?

FENIAN

Wait, I don't think…

SISK

Quiet! (*Back to* **FERRA**.) Good help, powerful help, is so hard to find in this world we live in. Wouldn't you agree that such a precious commodity as a blue mage deserves some form of payment?

FENIAN

I am not some piece of merchandise…

*(**SISK** raises her hand to slap **FENIAN**, but rethinks this move and walks closer to him instead.)*

SISK

If… when you leave me, I will have nothing left in my life. Let me at least have some gold to comfort my dark heart.

ELLIE

He isn't going anywhere. Fenian is going to be with me.

FERRA

The longer he stays here, the more likely he will be found out by the Magistrate.

ANNA

You can't be selfish about this, Ellie. You have to think of what is best for Fenian.

ELLIE

I know what is best… for both of us.

*(**ELLIE** walks over and pulls the gilded rope that sounds the bells. **SISK** hides as The **QUEEN**, the **MAGIS-TRATE**, and **ADEMAR** enter with several guards.)*

QUEEN

You have called, child?

ELLIE

I have decided, my Queen. I will marry Fenian.

QUEEN

Why, that is joyous news, Ellie, but this isn't the time to make such announcements. Perhaps you should have had a council with me first.

MAGISTRATE

Precisely, Your Majesty, we are on the search for Lorason's killer. *(Staring at **ELLIE**.)* Perhaps when all is said and done, we can make such an announcement.

ELLIE

No, Magistrate. The time is now. I am to marry Fenian.

FENIAN

*(To **ELLIE**.)* What are you doing?

ELLIE

*(To **FENIAN**.)* Trust me.

QUEEN

So be it. We will start the arrangements in the morning, but for now, our efforts must be used to find the young squire's killer.

*(**TOFOL** enters with **WREN** by his side.)*

TOFOL

Sorry to get here so late after the bells rang. These old bones don't move like they used to.

ADEMAR

You old craven! It had to be you. My Queen, while we all gather here, let us at least put this old man to trial.

TOFOL

Now see here, Sir Knight, it was decided that I was nowhere near the room when Lorason went missing. All the guards have been questioned by the Magistrate?

MAGISTRATE

Thoroughly. And not one of them is a mage. I would know.

TOFOL

I hate to say this, but one amongst us has to be the culprit, then.

ADEMAR

Who?

TOFOL

I think it is safe to say that I, Lady Ferra and her apprentice are to be ruled out.

ADEMAR

And why those two, sir?

FERRA

Because I am a green mage and Anna here is a red mage. Healing and Fire. Our powers could not create the ice used to kill Lorason.

MAGISTRATE

Do you hear this, your Majesty? We have had the Marble Castle infiltrated with dangerous beings!

ADEMAR

What about the demon? He could have been there when Lorason met his fate.

WREN

I was there when he died.

(Stunned silence.)

I saw the whole thing.

ELLIE

He did not just witness Lorason's death. He was the cause!

FENIAN

*(To **ELLIE**.)* You are telling the truth?

ELLIE

*(To **FENIAN**.)* I told you to trust me.

MAGISTRATE

I think it is time Lady Elisven told us all she knows.

QUEEN

Please, dear. What is it you have been keeping a

secret?

ELLIE

The demon Wren manipulated Lorason and Fenian into fighting each other. He was clouding their minds.

ANNA

It's true. I was there too when they were about to fight and even before that when they were confronting each other. I felt my mind become…

ELLIE

When Lorason attacked Fenian, his reaction caused the ice spikes. It was self-defense. Fenian didn't- doesn't even know how to control it.

MAGISTRATE

So a blue mage killed someone inside this castle? Do you see, my Queen, the dangers of keeping mages here? We must wipe out this threat. He was probably given orders from the necromancer downstairs.

ELLIE

It was an accident. Fenian never meant to…

ADEMAR

Enough!(*He draws his sword.*)I am sick of the Lady's games and I will take my vengeance on the boy! Come here and face me as you faced my squire!

ELLIE

Wren, stop this! You are manipulating him aren't you?

WREN

No, m'lady. I cannot use my powers while my master is near me.

TOFOL

So you did have a hand in this?

WREN

Master, please, I only acted in a way to protect you.

ELLIE

Enough, Wren. Drop the act.

ADEMAR

I have had enough talk from all of you.

(*ADEMAR rushes towards* **FENIAN**. **SISK** *leaps out of hiding and in a flourish of her black robes stands behind the* **QUEEN** *with a knife to her throat.*)

QUEEN

You really should rethink what you do here.

SISK

Quiet, your Grace. I would hate to have to bring you back after slicing your royal throat.

FERRA

Even if you walk out of here now, you will be hunted, Lady Sisk. You are threatening the life of a queen.

SISK

You threatened my livelihood by wanting to steal my Fenian away from me.

ELLIE

He was only worth something to you once you found out what he was capable of.

ADEMAR

I suggest you let our sovereign go, witch.

SISK

Fenian, collect our things. We will leave and never return. And in exchange for our safe departure, I will not harm the Queen. I think this is fair. Don't you, knight?

ADEMAR

I will see you die…

SISK

Fenian! Now!

(**FENIAN** *starts to go and gather the satchels and*

bags he had arrived with.)

TOFOL

Lady Sisk, I implore you to re-think what you do here. This is highly illegal and extremely amoral.

SISK

Do I seem like the type who cares about the morality of any given situation, old man? The Queen will help escort Fenian and I out of the city. Then, I will return her to you unscathed once we reach Poneleve.

ADEMAR

I think not!

*(As **FENIAN** crosses **ADEMAR**, the knight's sword is plunged into **FENIAN**'s stomach. There are gasps of horror. **ELLIE** rushes over to the fallen body. **SISK**, enraged, pushes the **QUEEN** aside and rushes towards **ADEMAR**, but is held back by **FERRA** and **ANNA**. Two guards try to take **ADEMAR** by the arms, but with a flourish are relieved of their own weapons.)*

QUEEN

Call in more guards! Seize The Knight, Ademar!

ELLIE

You killed him!

SISK

Who has murdered in cold blood now? You will answer for this, knight! I will see to it.

*(**ADEMAR** fights off two more guards before exiting, being pursued. Two more guards enter to tend to the **QUEEN**.)*

QUEEN

Guards, find that man and take him to the dungeons right away. He is to be executed for his crimes here today. (*She walks over and kneels next to **ELLIE**.*) He is gone? (***ELLIE** nods.*) Lady Sisk, I feel it is time for you to earn your redemption. Bring back your apprentice.

SISK

Let go of me! (*Taking a step away from **FERRA** and*

ANNA.) My Queen, I need a life to take in order to give life to the fallen.

ELLIE

Take Ademar's when he is caught.

SISK

It is best to do it as soon as possible. Ademar may be at the city gates or further by now.

QUEEN

Tofol, the amulet you were giving me. May we give it to the boy instead? Would it help him were he to come back?

TOFOL

I suppose, Your Majesty, but I meant that as a gift for you.

QUEEN

And I want to see my ward happy with her chosen love.

TOFOL

Very well, Your Majesty.

ELLIE

My Queen, before you perform such a grand gesture, please hear my confession.

QUEEN

Confession, child?

ELLIE

I must tell you the truth, the reason for all of this chaos. I must let you know why I will no longer be here in New Trale.

ANNA

Ellie, what are saying? Did you plan all this?

ELLIE

Not everything.

MAGISTRATE

Lady Elisven, I suggest you keep your thoughts quiet.

ELLIE

No longer, Magistrate. I want to be with Fenian. Our plan didn't involve me finding love, but here we are.

ANNA

You are in league with this sleazy degenerate?

MAGISTRATE

I beg your pardon, young lady!?

FERRA

Please let the Lady Elisven finish what she is saying. (*To **ELLIE**.*) I suggest you tell your whole story.

QUEEN

Go ahead, Ellie.

ELLIE

From when I was born, until I was six years of age, I was raised in Poneleve with the demons as my caretakers, other than my parents of course. Not being a male heir, a treaty was signed with New Trale that gave peace to Paydunor and gave this kingdom a ward and potential future ruler. I have truly loved my time here and will forever be indebted to you, Your Majesty, for all that you have taught me. However, I have been working with the Magistrate to find my way back to my kingdom ensuring his rule here.

ANNA

That is the grossest thing I have ever heard. I may be sick.

ELLIE

Another thing to break your heart, my Queen, is that I am a sympathizer for the creatures that are ruled by my family. I see their imprisonment as a plight that needs to end. And the Magistrate and I will stop at nothing to see the demons free.

MAGISTRATE

But what of the mage? The boy lying at your feet? He is an abomination and his kind must be annihilated. Our talks included a plan for the eradication of…

ELLIE

Never once have I agreed to your skewed view of the mages. He was caught in our plans and I hope that Lady Sisk will bring him back.

FERRA

In light of your true intentions, I think the queen must have some time to decide what she is to do.

SISK

If you want Fenian to return, my Queen, we must act immediately. There is no time.

TOFOL

I think Her Majesty deserves…

SISK

The more time passes the less chance of my apprentice…

ANNA

Why are we arguing? Is no one else disturbed by Ellie's confession?

QUEEN

I will give him my life.

(Pause. All is quiet.)

TOFOL

Your Majesty, please think about what you say.

QUEEN

I have thought about my death for some time now. Ellie, despite the things you say this day, I still love you with all my heart. You are the daughter I never had. To see you happy is all I ever wanted. If New Trale falls to the Magistrate's rule, I feel the mage's fate will be safe as long as you are in a seat of power. I give my waning life to the young man you love.

FERRA

I am still unconvinced that you are dying, Your Majesty. You may be giving up a longer life than you think.

QUEEN

If that is true, it is still my choice to make.

ELLIE

I don't know what to say…

QUEEN

Say nothing and rule justly.

ELLIE

You aren't heartbroken by what I've said?

QUEEN

I am. But your smile is worth the sacrifice.

*(**ELLIE** and the **QUEEN** embrace.)*

I love you Ellie.

SISK

It seems that the decision has been made. I need only two vials from my satchel and a book.

TOFOL

That is all?

SISK

Most of what I do in private homes is more for… show.

TOFOL

Charlatan…

SISK

I am so sick of being called that! Sure I add some flare to what I do, but…

ELLIE

Enough! Please, Lady Sisk. Before he is too far

gone.

SISK

Very well. Give me a moment to collect my things.

MAGISTRATE

I will accompany you, Lady Sisk. I wouldn't want you leaving before doing what you promised.

SISK

Of course, Magistrate. (*She exits with the* **MAGISTRATE**.)

TOFOL

Now, Wren, what to do with you? You played a part in all this and I cannot sit idly by and let your actions go unpunished.

WREN

Please, master. I was following orders from my lady here.

ELLIE

It is true, Tofol. He was only doing what I'd asked him to do.

TOFOL

Whom do you serve, Wren?

WREN

The future queen of Poneleve, sir. I can no longer be yours to command.

TOFOL

Very well. (*To the* **QUEEN**.) It seems both my apprentice and your ward had agendas we knew nothing about.

WREN

Please do not be angry with me, master.

TOFOL

I am afraid I no longer have that title, demon.

(**TOFOL** *extends his hand to* **WREN**. *The demon takes a moment and then shakes it. After a pause,* **WREN** *begins to take off his elaborate tail-coat.)*

No, Wren. Keep that. It was a gift. Wear it to remember our time together.

WREN

Thank you, sir. I will cherish this.

TOFOL

(*To the* **QUEEN**.) Here is your amulet. Yours to give to the Lady Elisven. (*He hands her the amulet from his sleeve.*) It was worn by my love, given to her by Lady Ferra. May it help with the young love we see here.

QUEEN

Thank you, Tofol. This is a generous gift.

TOFOL

Well, I feel I am no longer needed. I shall take my leave.

ANNA

Where will you go?

TOFOL

(*Pause.*) I won't journey too far. I feel as though a pint at a tavern in Riddon is calling my name. Perhaps I can warm these old bones at the bottom of a glass. Wren, would you walk me out one last time?

WREN

It would be an honor, sir.

(**WREN** *and* **TOFOL** *exit.* **SISK** *enters with the* **MAGIS-TRATE**. *She holds two small vials and a book.*)

SISK

Lay Fenian out and cross his arms on his chest. Where has the old man gone?

FERRA

He just left.

SISK

Oh, well, I didn't want to say goodbye to him anyway. Old fool. Why don't you, Magistrate, stand by the boy in case he wakes violently.

MAGISTRATE

I will do no such thing! That mage could awake and kill me.

ANNA

I will stand next to him.

SISK

Very well. (*She hands* **ANNA** *a vial.)* This is the restorative.

ELLIE

That's the bottle labeled water.

SISK

Of course it's labeled water. Would I label a life saving drought with its actual name? How stupid do you think I am child?

ANNA

I have a guess to that question.

SISK

Now… I forget your name…

ANNA

It's…

SISK

Unimportant, yes, you're right. Anyway, pour that vial's contents into Fenian's mouth when I give you a signal. (*Turning to the* **QUEEN**.) This is highly potent poison. Its contents will lull you to sleep and kill you all in an instant. It will be as if you fell asleep and never woke up. (**SISK** *hands the* **QUEEN** *the vial.*) When I say drink, you drink. Are my instructions clear, Your Majesty? (*The* **QUEEN** *nods.*) Good. Oh… I'm sorry for holding a knife to you. I was a bit desperate and to tell you the truth, I haven't eaten all day and I get a little crazy when I'm hungry. You know how it is.

FERRA

And the book?

SISK

When our Queen drinks, I will start reading the blessing. I will signal you… uh… girl… to empty the vial into Fenian's mouth.

ANNA

Is this really all there is to it?

SISK

Yes. Shall we begin.

ELLIE

Just a moment, please.

*(**SISK** nods. **ELLIE** stands and walks over to the **QUEEN**.)*

ELLIE

Let me just say thank you, one more time.

QUEEN

Of course, my dear.

ELLIE

I heard all you had to say and I will take your kind words with me. I have been selfish.

QUEEN

No, dear, you were following your heart. You mustn't…

ELLIE

I can't be selfish anymore.

*(**ELLIE** takes the vial from the **QUEEN** and drinks its contents.)*

QUEEN

Ellie! No!

*(Almost instantly **ELLIE** falls to the floor. The Queen rushes to her side. **SISK** begins to read pointing at **ANNA**.)*

SISK

To the Three we pray,

By light of this day,

To bring back from death,

With another life we pay.

From darkness return,

Guided by flame's true burn,

Across the fields of death,

Bring back to us with life-giving breath!

(For a moment there is nothing. No movement. Then **FENIAN** *begins to stir. He sits up violently. He then shakes his head as if he is waking up from a deep slumber.)*

FENIAN

What happened?

ANNA

It actually worked?

FERRA

Quick, Your Majesty, the amulet.

(The **QUEEN***, sobbing over* **ELLIE***'s body, hands* **FERRA** *the amulet.* **FERRA** *places it around* **FENIAN***'s neck.)*

FENIAN

I heard Lady Sisk's voice in the dark and then woke up. I was stabbed. Did I pass out?

FERRA

You died, Fenian. Lady Elisven gave her life to bring you back.

FENIAN

No. Why would she do that...

ANNA

She loved you. That can make people do stupid things. You know, like, killing yourself.

(The **QUEEN** *collapses next to* **ELLIE***'s body.* **FERRA** *rushes over to her.)*

FERRA

She's dead.

FENIAN

How did she die? What killed her?

FERRA

She died of a broken heart. *(To SISK.)* Quick, get another vial. *(SISK exits.)* Fenian, move Ellie's body out of the way. Lay her next to the Queen here. *(FENIAN moves ELLIE's body.)* Now give me the amulet. *(FENIAN hands it over.)* Do you feel any different while not wearing it?

FENIAN

No. Not at all.

FERRA

That's good. I will place it around Lady Elisven's neck. *(She does so.)* Maybe it will help her.

(SISK enters with the vial and hands it to FENIAN.)

SISK

You know what to do?

FENIAN

Yes, m'Lady.

SISK

Good boy. Now all stand back. *(SISK opens the book again and reads as FENIAN pours the vial into ELLIE's mouth.)*

To the Three we pray,

By light of this day,

To bring back from death,

With another life we pay.

From darkness return,

Guided by flame's true burn,

Across the fields of death,

Bring back to us with life-giving breath!

*(For a moment there is nothing. No movement. Then **ELLIE** begins to stir. She sits up violently. She then shakes her head as if she is waking up from a deep slumber.)*

FENIAN

Ellie?

ELLIE

Fenian?*(The two embrace, unconcerned with the company around them.)* What happened?

FENIAN

The Queen… she…

ELLIE

*(She sees the **QUEEN'**s body next to her.)* Oh no. My Queen…

FERRA

She knew it was her time. I could not see it, but she knew. The shock of you taking your own life was what pushed her over the edge.

ELLIE

So it was my fault she died.

ANNA

She wanted you to be happy, Ellie. She gave her life so that you could live.

ELLIE

Magistrate, call for guards to carry our Queen to her chambers.

MAGISTRATE

Of course, Lady Elisven. *(He starts to exit but stops short of leaving the stage.)* I would be remiss if I didn't ask…

ELLIE

After the Queen's burial, I will leave and New Trale will be yours to rule as you wish.

MAGISTRATE

Very good, my Lady.

SISK

My good Magistrate, a moment? Perhaps the new regime may find a place at court for woman of my talents?

MAGISTRATE

You have indeed proven yourself twice today. I think we could find a place for you at court.(*Exits.*)

SISK

Fenian?

FENIAN

Yes, m'Lady?

SISK

I release you from your obligations as my apprentice.

FENIAN

M'Lady?

SISK

I have no need for a second rate ice salesman. Enjoy your demon queen. (*She exits following after the **Magistrate**.*)

FENIAN

Just as kind leaving me as she was when finding me.

ELLIE

Fenian, will you stay with me?

FERRA

I think it would be wiser if he came with Anna and me. With the Magistrate in power, it will not be safe for the three of us. We can meet you in Riddon in a few days after you settle matters here.

FENIAN

If you need me here, I will stay.

ELLIE

Lady Ferra is right. Go with her and stay safe.

FERRA

Lady Elisven, I am in your employ should you need me. I do not share your sympathy for the demons your people rule over, but I trust you will be a competent ruler.

ELLIE

Thank you, Lady Ferra.

FERRA

Fenian, I will meet with you outside. I wish good luck to befall you both. (*She exits.*)

ANNA

(*Walking to* **ELLIE**.) You are a conniving and secretive demon sympathizer… but I can't help but have respect for you. (*She hugs* **ELLIE**.) If he ever hurts you…

ELLIE

You'll have my back.

ANNA

Every time. (*She exits.*)

FENIAN

So I'll see you in Riddon?

ELLIE

Yes. Then we can start our next adventure.

(*The two kiss. Fenian turns and exits. Guards enter and start to take the* **QUEEN**'s *body off stage.* **ELLIE** *stops them.*)

It all went according to plan. You and I are free.

(**ELLIE** *kisses the* **QUEEN**'s *forehead. The guards take the* **QUEEN**'s *body off stage as the lights fade.*)

Curtain.

Made in the
USA
Columbia, SC